How to Ask a Girl Out

How to Ask a Girl Out

TABLE OF CONTENT

FOREWORD

You will find life a lot easier if you take time to study the art of asking a girl out. That does not mean trying out all the suggestions you get from friends and colleagues, who will be only too happy to share their ideas. Every female is different, and you need to take the time to get to know her personality as well as her likes and dislikes, before you progress to asking her out. It will take time to get to know her, especially if she is reserved, or a very private person. This EBook will provide you with practical advice on how you can get to know her and convince her to go out with you.

This is not a quick-fix solution. You will need to be prepared to put in the time and effort if you want to succeed. This is a step-by-step process, which will help you to understand how the female mind works and allow you to communicate with your prospective date successfully. Your approach has to be adaptable depending on the girl's personality. If she is outgoing and approachable, you can just go ahead and ask her out. However, if she is shy and reserved, you will need to be more thoughtful about your approach, or you may frighten her off completely. This EBook will introduce you to the secrets that will help you to improve your chances of success when you ask for a date.

Changes in behavior and society have made it much easier for individuals to strike up relationships. It is not unusual these days for a relationship to start within a matter of hours or days from the first meeting. However, in some cases it may take a lot more communication and persuasion to get the girl to accept a date as an opportunity for getting to know each other better.

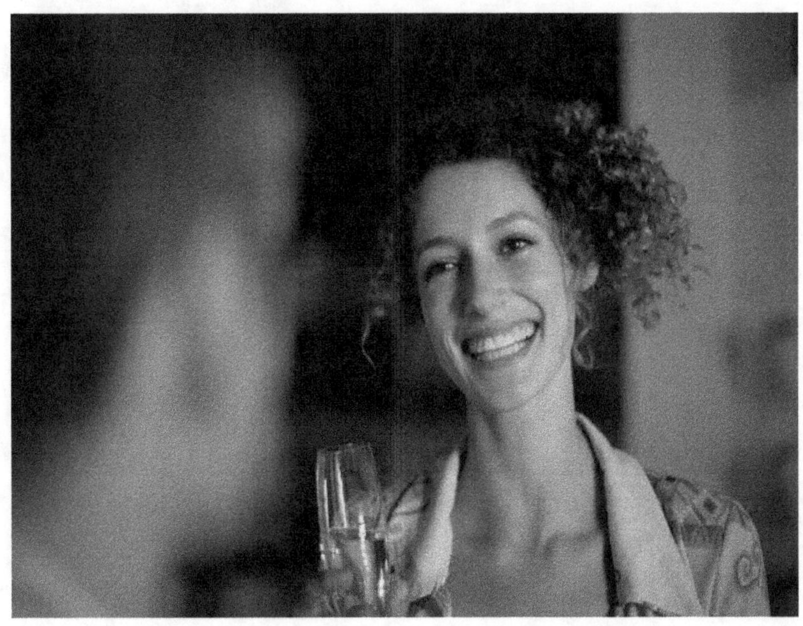

Chapter 01

"Different Types of Girls"

In this chapter I will tell you about the types of girls that you are likely to meet. I will also tell you how you should go about getting to know them better.

Synopsis

- ❖ **Girls Who Have a Calm Nature**
- ❖ **Girls Who Are Bold**
- ❖ **Girls Who Are Flirty**
- ❖ **Girls Who Are Less Attractive**
- ❖ **Girls Who Are Boring**

I will tell you how to recognize the different categories of girls, so you can choose one that is compatible with you and your environment, behavior and habits.

Girls Who Have a Calm Nature

If you are looking for a long-term or possibly a life-time partner to settle down with, you should look for this type of girl.

She will have a serious out-look and approach to life and have little interest in things frivolous. She is a 'one-man woman' and will expect the man to wear the trousers in a relationship. She is likely to be compliant and willing to please. However, she does have standards and habits that are set in stone and will be almost impossible to change. She will judge you by her standards and expect you to have similar expectations and goals in life.

Girls Who Are Bold

These girls appear to be and are very different from calm girls. However, they have an underlying seriousness when it comes to a love relationship, and they will expect commitment from you.

These girls enjoy flirting. They prefer it when they are the center of your attention. They are very outgoing and fun to be with, but you need to be aware of their invisible boundaries. They will cut you off very quickly if you overstep the mark. Remaining faithful is an essential in a relationship with these girls. They may appear possessive as they can display a need to hang out with you all the time.

Girls Who Are Flirty

You may often come across girls who are flirty, but very shallow. They often jump from one relationship to another, or have several ongoing at the same time. You should never expect more than a short but often exhilarating fling with these girls.

They are usually very attractive and belief it's their right to be admired and pampered by boys. They are often referred to a 'man's woman' because they may not connect with other females easily. They may always expect you to pay on a date, and you will need to shower them with gifts.

They are usually accused of only being interested in what they can get out of any relationship, so you can expect to be replaced once the first initial excitement of the relationship calms down. They detest boredom and normality.

Girls Who Are Less Attractive

These girls may not have the looks, but they do have a warm and very supportive nature. They can very easily become your life-long best friend, rather than a date.

They believe that they have nothing to offer in the attraction's stakes and can become very wary with boys, who are attracted to them. They mistrust the intention of boys that offer flowery compliments and make romantic gestures.

They have a mind of their own and expect boys to be more attracted to their mind, than their looks. They put friendship much higher up in the relationship stakes than love. You may need to do the same and forget about romantic gestures and dates.

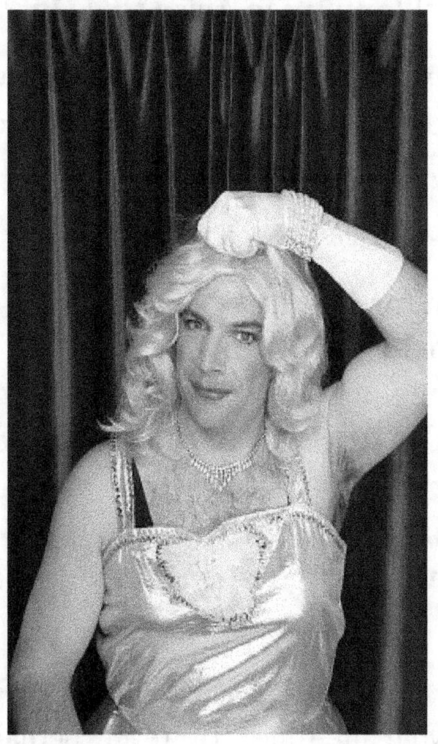

Girls Who Are Boring

Coming into contact with girls who are boring is not uncommon. That usually means that you have no shared interests, on which to build a relationship.

During your initial contact, the girl may seem fun and outgoing. However, once you've covered all the get to know you bits. You will likely run out of things to talk about. As you have no shared interests or hobbies the relationship will quickly stall. It may be better not to start a relationship in the first place.

Chapter 02

"Planning to Ask a Girl Out?"

There are several things you need to plan when you are going to ask a girl out. This chapter will guide you through the planning.

Synopsis

- ❖ **Reason for Failure**
- ❖ **Plan to do Something Exciting**
- ❖ **Plan the Logistics of Your Date in Advance**
- ❖ **Take it as Read, That You Have to do the Asking**
- ❖ **Choosing the Right Moment**
- ❖ **Knowing When the Time is Right to ask Her Out.**

You are likely to come across some tough situations throughout your life-time. However, perhaps one of the toughest will be getting it right, when you ask a girl out on a date. You are hoping she will say yes straight away. However, you may not always be that lucky and she may say no, or make excuses as to why she cannot go out with you.

Here are some tips on how you can get the girl to say yes to your request for a date.

Reason for Failure

If you are a stranger to the girl, you are asking out, the chances are she is more likely to say no. You could be 'Jack the Ripper' for all she knows. Her response will likely be an act of self-preservation that has little to do with you. She will be applying what she has been taught since early childhood 'not to talk, or go with strangers'

You should not allow a rejection to dent your self-confidence. You need to take things slowly and spend some time as acquaintances, getting to know each other. Once she gets to know and starts to feel comfortable with you, she is much more likely to say yes.

Plan to Do Something Exciting

Choose something fun activities you can do with a group of friends. That gives you the opportunity to invite the girl to join your group as a friend. You then have a non-threatening opportunity to relax and interact so you can get to know each other better.

If you succeed in getting the girl to hang out with you and some friends, you will find it much easier to ask her on a date. She is more likely to say yes, because she has seen that you can be a fun guy.

Be spontaneous, and don't be afraid to show you have a caring side. Show her you are intelligent and can talk about topics other than what's going on at school or at home. Talk about subjects or hobbies that really interest you, and take time to find out what she likes and dislikes.

It is all about natural and free flowing communication and getting to know about each other.

Plan the Logistics of Your Date in Advance

Plan ahead and know what you intend to do on the date. Then when you ask her if she is free that evening, you can tell her what you have planned and ask if that is OK with her. If she has already said she is free that night, she is unlikely to say no. If she sees you are willing to compromise about what you want to do during the date, it will help to win you brownie points.

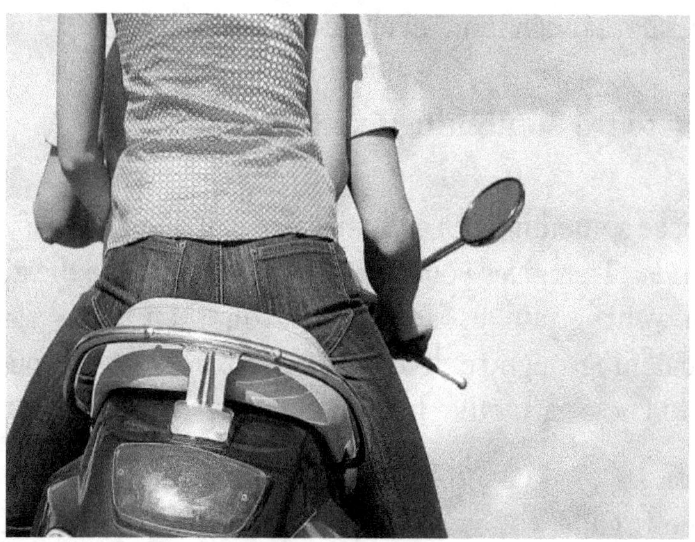

However, if after saying she is free, she then starts to make excuses why she cannot go on the date with you. You should accept it as a good sign, she is not attracted to you.

Alternatively, if she says, she already has plans for the evening you want to take her out; you can try some charm and gentle persuasion. If she knows you are a fun person to be with, and she is attracted to you, you may get her to change her plans. Or you can ask her what night would be OK with her.

Take it as Read That You Have to do the Asking.

Don't labor under the misapprehension that a girl will ask you out on a date. Contrary to a popular belief, there are only a very small number of girls who will ask you out. If you don't want to miss out, then be prepared to be the one that asks for a date.

Choosing the Right Moment

Making sure you choose the right moment to ask a girl on a date is important. If you rush in and ask her before she has had the chance to get to know you, she will say no. It may take several meetings as friends before you find the right moment. You need to be patient, use your instincts and learn to read the signs she is giving you, and you should know instinctively when she is ready to progress to dating.

Knowing When the Time is Right to Ask Her Out

There are several signs that may indicate that the girl is ready to go out on a date with you. In addition to the way she looks at you and her body language, you may notice a more intimate tone in her conversation with you.

She will show an interest in you, even when you talk about something boring or are saying very little. You need to rely on your instinct and natural ability to know when the time is right to ask her for a date.

Chapter 03

"Ideas for Being Romantic"

If you want to ask a girl out on a date, you should approach her with some style and romance. The advice in this chapter will help you to bring out the romantic side of your personality.

Synopsis

❖ **Don't be Afraid to Show your Feminine Side or Caring Nature**
❖ **Believe in Yourself**
❖ **Sit Down and Make a List**
❖ **Make the First Move**
❖ **Communications**
❖ **Be There for Her when She Needs You**
❖ **Make Sure She Notices You**

Having a girl as a friend is one thing; it is the moving on to a romantic relationship that can be the difficult part. Making a smooth transition will be easy if you approach it in the right way. What you say, and the way you behave, when you ask a girl out, can be the key to your success or your failure.

Don't be Afraid to Show your Feminine Side or Caring Nature

If you are really interested in a girl, you need to let her know. That often means toning down your 'macho' attitude and behavior and letting her see you have a softer and more caring nature. If you come across as having too much testosterone, you risk frightening or turning the girl off, and she will make excuses not to go out with you.

Many of the male populations are reluctant to admit that they have a feminine side, especially in front of other males. However, the best way to get the girl to go out on a date is to show her you do have a sensitive and caring nature. If you do this, and she continues to turn you down, then you should forget her and find another girl to ask out.

Believe in Yourself

You may not be the most attractive male on the planet, but you may not be the ugliest. You need to be strong in the belief that you do have something to offer a girl. However, you do need to find the right balance between being self-confident or being over-bearing, if you want to be successful in attracting the girl.

If like most males starting out on the dating game, you think you don't have a romantic bone in your body, you may be surprised. Following a few simple steps can introduce you to your romantic side.

Sit Down and Make a List

If you are not good at remembering things, you can write them down in a list. Girls are well impressed if you remember their birthday, or special occasions such as anniversaries, without having to be reminded. The minimum you should do is send her a card, but you will gain a lot more brownie points if you send flowers, chocolates or take her out for a nice meal to celebrate.

You can also use your list to make a note of her likes and dislikes such as does she have a favorite perfume, what is her favorite color and so on? It will save you a whole lot of grief if you choose something she really likes as a gift for those special occasions.

Make the First Move

Knowing when your relationship with a girl is ready to move on to the next stage can be tricky. As many girls will be reluctant to take the initiative, it is up to you to make the first move. If you over-step the mark, by being too passionate too quickly, you can destroy the relationship. You need to start off by saying goodbye with a wave or a casual kiss on the cheek. You can hold hands while walking, or while sitting in the cinema. The more you get to know her the easier you will find it is to read the signs. She will let you know when she is ready to progress the relationship.

Communication

Communication plays a very important part in any relationship. It is an excellent tool that provides the opportunity for the couple to find out what makes each other tick. The conversations should be natural and should be geared as much to listen and learning, as they are about talking. Initially, the girl may appear to be shy or unwilling to talk about herself, talking about interests or hobbies you have in common will help her to relax.

You can try to draw her out by asking questions. However, you should take care that you don't make her feel like she is being interrogated.

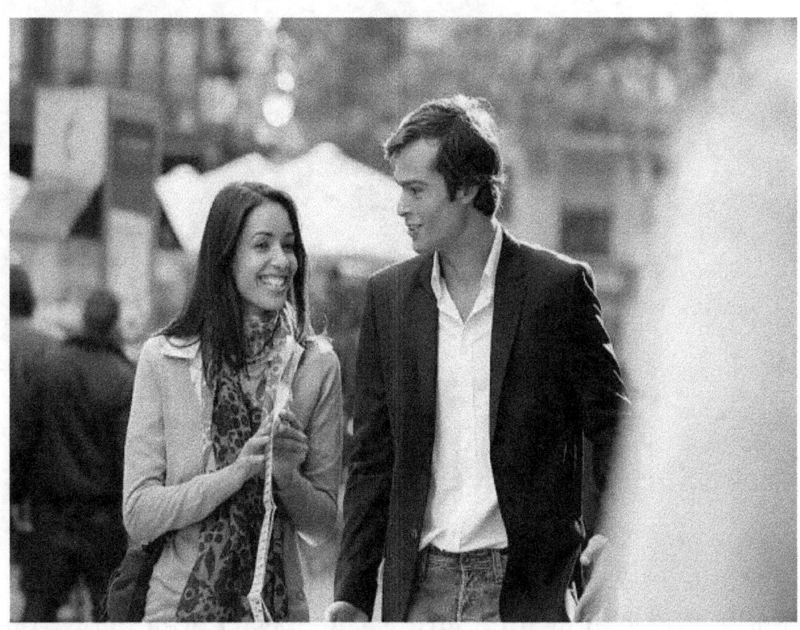

Be There for Her When She Needs You

If your girl is upset for any reason, or just feels unwell, you need to bring out your caring side and be there for her. You may not be able to do anything to cure a physical ailment, but you can provide emotional support. Just by being there and listening shows that you really care and that can help to improve her emotional state.

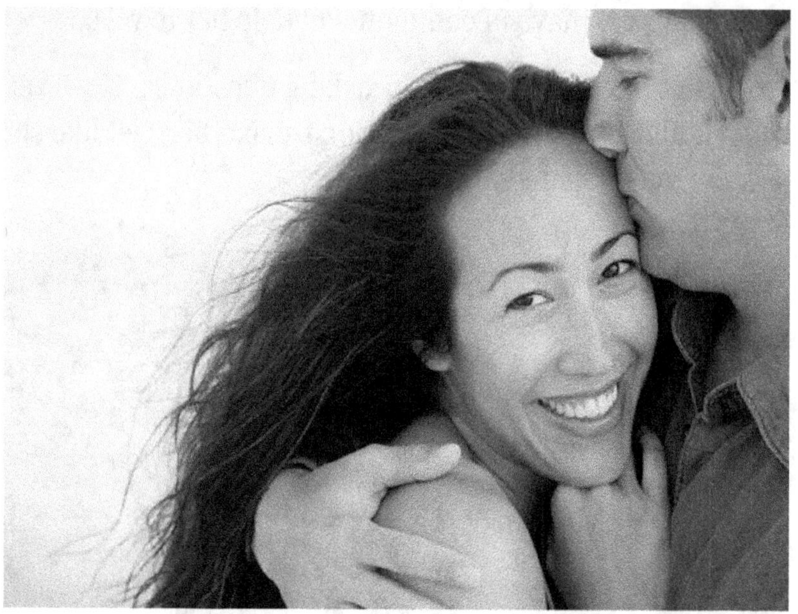

Make Sure She Notices You

There is little point in you wasting your time and energy putting on a show for a girl, is she doesn't even know you are there. You need to make sure your actions involve something she is interested in and ask her to get involved or to give you her opinion on what you intend doing. Unfortunately for some, that does mean you need to talk to her and get to know her first, before trying to impress.

Chapter 04

"Tips for Asking a Girl Out"

If you are asking girls for a date and being rejected, then you should read the tips in this chapter to find out what you are doing wrong.

Synopsis

- ❖ **Presentation and Punctuality are Necessities**
- ❖ **Remaining Calm and Happy**
- ❖ **Compliment Her and Make the Environment Interested**
- ❖ **Follow Your Instincts**
- ❖ **Always Stay Positive and Thoughtful**
- ❖ **Show Your Intent and Passion**
- ❖ **Look For Positive Dates**

Society takes a much more casual view of dating habits these days than used to be the case in our parents and grandparents days. It was almost unheard of for individuals to have multiple relationships ongoing at the same time. Dating was taken seriously and when it became a longer term relationship is usually ended in marriage.

Whereas, today it is not that unusual for individuals to frequently change dating partners, or have several at the same time. It is much less likely that individuals will enter into a marriage with their first dating partner. Unfortunately, this modern practice of trying out multiple dates in the search for the right partner can have disastrous consequences of a criminal nature.

Preparation and Punctuality are Necessities

Preparing for a first date is important. If you want to make a good impression you have to start by considering how you will look. Ask yourself what your date is likely to think of the way you present yourself? Will she be able to see that you have made an effort? Making an effort with how you appear, especially on the first date will help to create a favorable impression.

Punctuality for your first date is just as important as your appearance. Even being a few minutes' late, sends out the wrong signals before your date has even started. You are better off planning to be at your meeting place a few minutes early.

Remaining Calm and Happy

Try to remain calm and don't let your nerves show on a first date. If you are feeling a bit uptight, taking a few deep breaths can help to relax you before your date turns up.

If you are someone who is easily wound up by poor service, then you need to select the venue for your date carefully. You will not win any brownie points if you lose your temper or create a fracas about the littlest thing. Remaining cool, calm and collected if you are justified in making a complaint creates a good impression and shows that you can act responsibly.

Don't Shy Away from Giving Her Compliments

Any individual, especially a female who says she doesn't appreciate a compliment is lying. However, the compliment does have to be sincere or your date will likely pick up on it. Although this is sometimes an area where you may need to rely on your tact and sensitivity, especially if she asks you what you think about her new dress, or a new hairstyle and you hadn't noticed. She will not thank you for your honesty if you tell her you hate it.

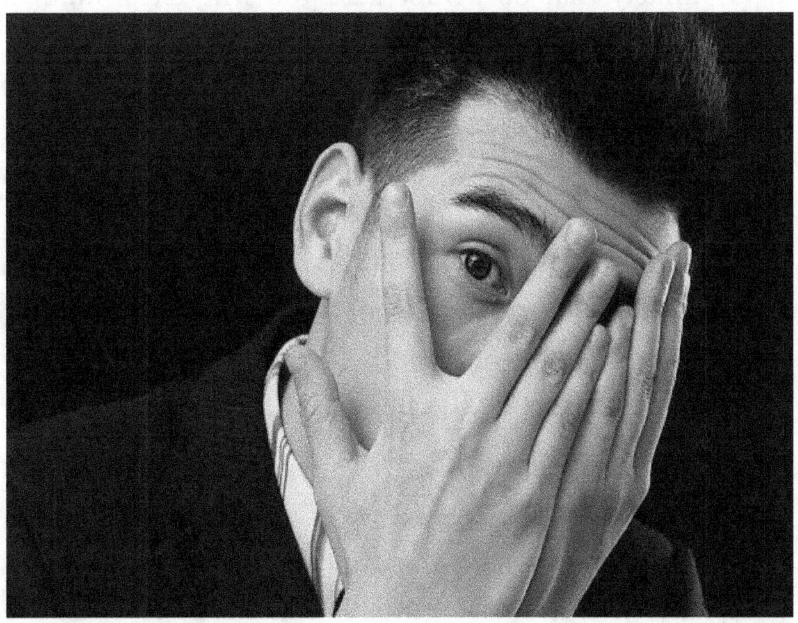

Actively listening to what your date has to say and accepting her right to have her own opinions, helps to show that you value and respect your date. If you allow your attention to drift, or constantly interrupt to impose your own opinions over hers, you are unlikely to get a second date.

You need to take responsibility for keeping the conversation flowing as naturally as you can. You can do that by ensuring there are no long gaps in the conversation. Having a mental list of topics you can introduce into the conversation, that you know will interest your date, helps to avoid those uncomfortable silences.

Rely on Your Instincts and Tell the Truth

It is unlikely that on a first date you will get around to telling your girl all your deepest, darkest secrets. However, there are some things that you need to be up front about and you will know instinctively what they are. If you want the relationship to continue and develop beyond the first date you need to tell her. She can then decide if she wants to continue dating you. You need to think carefully about what would happen if she finds out about your secret from another source, before you get around to telling her. It will get harder to tell her if you keep putting it off.

On the other hand if she asks you a direct question, you can always lie. If you do you are likely to feel guilty about lying and when it does eventually come out you will have to explain why you lied. That can be enough to finish your relationship.

Remain Positive Despite Bad Experiences

If you can get through life without having to deal with a rejection in the dating game, you will be very lucky. Nearly everyone will have at least one, if not more poor dating experiences at some point in their life. You just have to learn what you can from it and move on. You have to accept that life is not a 'bed of roses' and it is not always your fault that it didn't work out.

If you think you were even partially responsible for the breakdown of the date, then you can take steps to ensure that the same things don't ruin any of your future dates. You need to remain positive about finding the right date for you in the future.

Committed to Finding a Potential Life-Time Partner

If you are committed to finding a life-time partner as opposed to a girl for casual dating, you need to be clear in your own mind about what you are looking for. You also need to be upfront with the girl, as she may not feel the same way as you do about a life-time relationship.

There are some girls out there who would be willing to commit to a life-time partner for any number of reasons. However, unless you have spent time getting to know each other first, which usually means dating. There are no guarantees that you will be compatible or that a life-time partnership will survive.

Positive Dating Experiences

If you are new to the dating game or are returning after a long period of time, it can be a daunting prospect. You will need to brush up on your knowledge and techniques if you want to find a good dating partner.

Spend some time people watching to see others in action and talk to friends and other people who may have just gone or are going through the same looking for a date experience. They will no doubt be a good source of advice and tips on how to go about it.

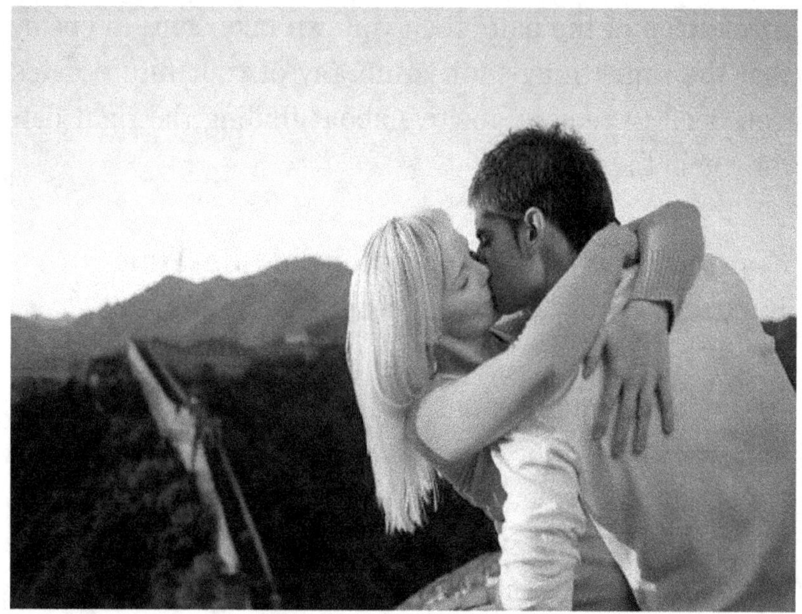

Chapter 05

"Five Rules for Asking a Girl Out"

In this chapter I am going to tell you the five golden rules that you should use when you ask a girl out.

Synopsis

- ❖ **Do Not Call Her Immediately**
- ❖ **Do Not Ask Her for a Date Straight Away**
- ❖ **Make Your Date More Fun than Stress**
- ❖ **Just Tell Her Your Plans Instead Of Asking Her**
- ❖ **Convince Your Girl**

It can be quite nerve racking to decide on the best way to ask a girl out. You need to consider a number of things, but these are the five rules you should always remember.

Do Not Call Her Immediately

Once you have your hands on the girl's phone number, don't call her straight away. If you appear too eager, she may think you are pressurizing her, and she may be put off you altogether.

Give her time to get used to the idea that you will be phoning her, but don't leave it too long or someone else may beat you to it. Usually, waiting for twenty-four to forty-eight hours is best.

Do Not Ask Her for a Date Straight Away

When you do get around to phoning, don't just jump into asking her out on a date. Spend some time chatting about life in general, or a topic that interests you both. If your instincts are telling you that you need to get to know each other a bit better before dating, arrange to meet for coffee or a lunch just as friends.

Alternatively, if you are arranging any type of group get together, you tell her she is welcome to come along. That way, you are not actually inviting her on a date, but it gives you the opportunity to get to know her better if she does come.

Make Your Date More Fun than Stress

Some people can make such a big deal out of their first date, they forget to have fun. Your girl will be much more impressed if you are relaxed and can show her that you are enjoying her company and whatever it is you are doing.

If you are stressing out about making sure the date is a success, you are likely to be trying too hard and that doesn't create a good impression and can be just as bad as being over-confident and blasé about the situation.

When choosing a venue or activity for your first date stick to something within your comfort zone. You will have enough nervous energy to contend with, without having the stress that comes from dealing with a new environment or activity at the same time.

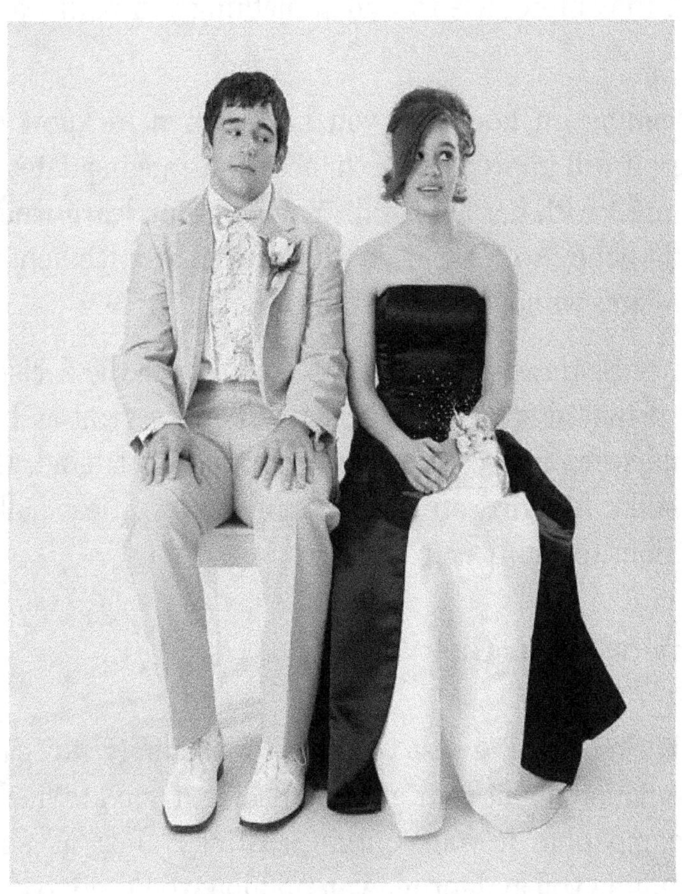

Just Tell Her Your Plans Instead Of Asking Her

It is very easy to get it wrong when you are choosing what to do and where to go on a first date. Someone has to take the initiative, and that should be you. Have some ideas in mind of what you would like to do, but tell your date what you're thinking about. Providing she does not object or make alternative suggestions, you should go ahead and make the arrangements.

If your suggestions do not meet with your girl's approval, ask her what she would like to do instead. You may both need to compromise to find something you both want to do.

Depending on how well you have gotten to know each other, it will improve your chances of arranging dates that will meet with her approval. You will soon learn whether she is happy to let you go ahead with arrangements for your dates without first consulting her.

Many girls these days expect an equal say in the decisions, and if they don't get it, they may perceive you as being domineering and controlling.   On the other hand, there are still a few girls around who are happy to leave all the decisions to you.

Convince Your Girl

Your first date gives you the opportunity to gather information about your girl and decide if you are likely to be compatible if you continue dating. Just as she is examining you and forming an opinion, you need to do the same with her personality. If you find that your opinions are conflicting about the small unimportant things, then you may have serious differences when it comes to the important life decisions. Compromising may not be an option unless both parties are willing.

Chapter 06

"Mistakes to Avoid When Asking A Girl Out"

There are some common mistakes that you should avoid when you asking a girl out. In this chapter I will tell you what those mistakes are.

Synopsis

- ❖ **Negative Thinking**
- ❖ **Don't Chase a Girl Who Is Not Interested In You**
- ❖ **Control your Insecurity and Jealousy**
- ❖ **Fear of Rejection**

Knowing how to impress a girl is often not enough. If you want to be successful you need to know the pitfalls and how to avoid them. This chapter will tell you more about the pitfalls to avoid.

Negative Thinking

Whether you consciously or unconsciously allow yourself to think negative thoughts, it will show up in your body language. If your date is perceptive enough to read your body language or picks up on your negativity through your conversation, that alone will put your date off. In many cases it can also prevent you from asking girls out on a date. The only one that can get rid of that negativity is you. You need to concentrate on what you have got, and your best features and eliminate the negative thoughts to improve your self-confidence.

Don't Chase a Girl Who Is Not Interested In You

One of the worst mistakes you can make is to keep pushing for a date when the girl has already turned you down. If she really isn't interested in you and you keep pushing she could perceive that you are stalking her. That could become a serious problem and get you into a lot of trouble.

You need to take what she is saying at face value and if she rejects your request for a date, back off. You need to turn your attentions elsewhere.

You need to be perceptive to whether the girl is interested, but is just playing hard to get by saying no when you first ask her out. If she starts ignoring you, and try's to avoid your company, you can be pretty sure she meant no when she said it. If she doesn't try and avoid you, or continues to talk to you, it might be worth waiting a while and trying again.

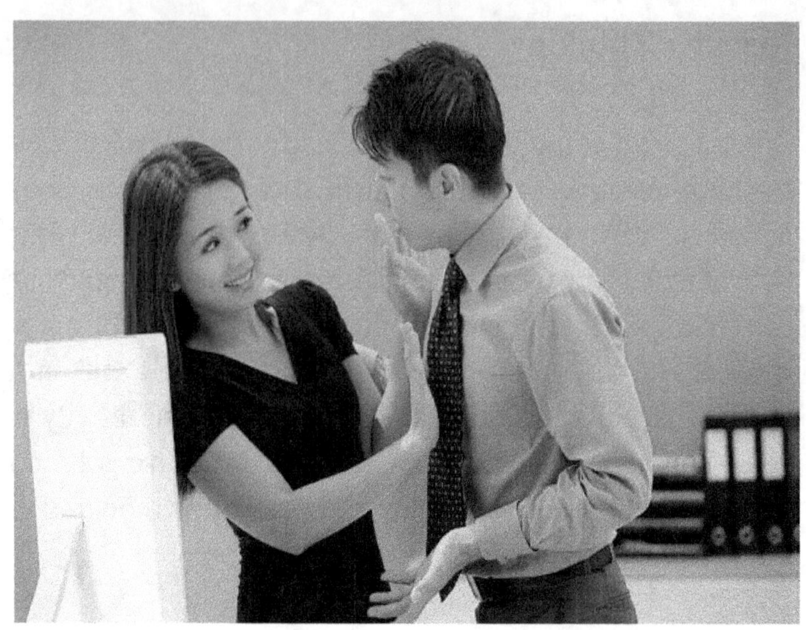

Control your Insecurity and Jealousy

Another often unforgivable mistake is to become jealous and insecure about your relationship. If you start being moody when she talks to other blokes, or you complain about her spending time with her girlfriends, you are on a slippery slope. Once it starts it usually only gets worse. You need to constantly remind yourself that your girl is not your possession, and she is with you because she wants to be.

Fear of Rejection

Rejection by a girl can dent your self-confidence and your ego. Usually if it's just your ego, you already think a lot of yourself and will convince yourself that it was her and not you, so no real harm done.

On the other hand, if your self-confidence takes a real knock you may find it harder to get up the courage to ask another girl out. You can always talk it through with someone you really trust that can help you to see it is not the end of the world and support you while you move on. The longer you leave it to move on, the harder it will be.

Chapter 07

"The First Impression Is a Lasting Impression"

Synopsis

- ❖ **Be Aware of Your Body Language**
- ❖ **Keep Some Secrets of Your Personality And Reveal Slowly**
- ❖ **Take Control of Your Date**
- ❖ **Be Funny and Have Fun**

If you are looking for shortcuts to impress a girl, you are wasting your time. They may be attracted to you, but are unlikely to fall at your feet without some effort on your part. However, first impressions do count and if you make a poor first impression you will have to work all the harder to change it.

Be Aware of Your Body Language

Be self-aware and know what your body language is saying about you. It is possible for a girl to tell a lot about you from your body language, before you approach or speak to her.

Watching other people and thinking about what their body language is saying to you, can help you to become more aware of you come across.

Keep Some Secrets of Your Personality and Reveal Slowly

Getting to know each other takes time and we all tend to be on our best behavior until we know the person better. That is OK, unless you are hiding a deep dark secret side to your personality.

It is easy to make the excuse that you didn't want to frighten her off on the first date, but she may feel more aggrieved if she finds out you have not been truthful with her from the start.

Take Control of Your Date

You have asked the girl out so you can expect to have some control on what you do and where you go. The girl may well be happy to sit back and let you take charge, but you take that for granted at your peril.

You need to remember that you are both equal and you both have a right to your own opinions. On the first date especially, you are getting to know about each other, so there should not really be any reason for debates, heated or otherwise. Steer the conversation to keep it away from what could be controversial subject until you know a bit more about each other.

Be Funny and Have Fun

If you have taken time to get to know each other as friends before going on a date, you will probably find it is a lot easier to be natural in each other company and you can relax and just have fun.

If it is a blind date, or you haven't had the chance to get to know each other you will likely be more uptight. It is not the best time to try out a new restaurant or venue you haven't been to before. The more familiar you both are with the surroundings the easier it will be to concentrate on each other and relax.

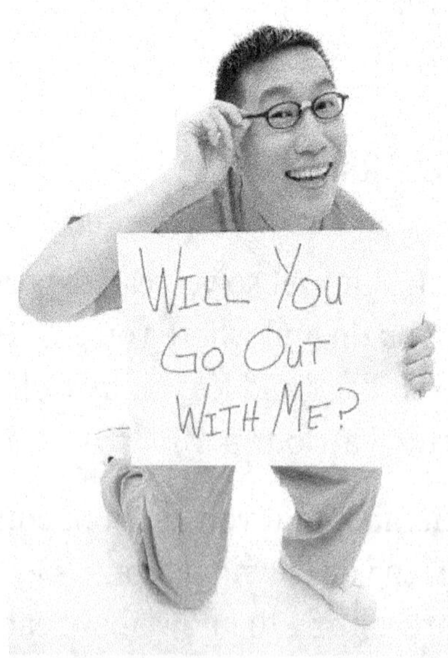

Wrapping up

Asking a girl out requires some sensitivity and skill that will come with practice. You are like to have some good and some bad experiences. You need to learn from the good ones and put the bad ones behind you so you can move on.

You should never let a bad experience dent your confidence because that is the key to getting your next date. Girls are more attracted to confident and assured males.

Not all girls are out for what they can get out of a relationship. However, if you do meet one that is very material orientated and start to date her, you will need deep pockets to keep the relationship going. Unless you run out of money, you may find she is hard to break up with, or she may quickly move on when she finds someone who can give her more. You need to decide what type of girl you are looking for.

This EBook has been written to provide you with an insight into how you can improve your ability to get dates. Unfortunately, as human beings are all different and you will rarely find two people who are immediately in tune with each other's personalities, you do need to build up some knowledge of the girl before she is likely to go out with you. This EBook will help to guide you in the right direction.

This EBook also attempts to give you an insight into the female psyche, but as I am sure you often heard said, "who can understand a women's mind"? The answer is probably not you, but it can be fun trying. So why not have some fun?